Rebuilding the Pyramids
(Poems of Healing in a Sick World)

By Mike Amado

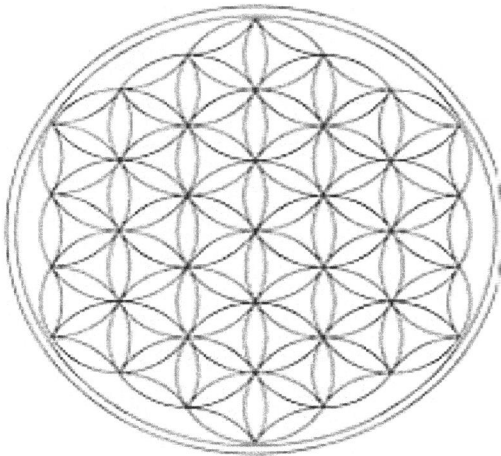

Ibbetson Street Press

ISBN 978-0-578-00041-1

Artwork:

Book designed by Steve Glines
Front cover collage assembled by Mike Amado,
contains images culled from *"The Da Vinci Enigma Tarot"*
by Caitlin Matthews, Saint Martin's Press 2005,
images originally drawn by Leonardo Da Vinci
"Spiral" by Barbara G. Barker

Distributed by

IBBETSON STREET PRESS
25 SCHOOL STREET
SOMERVILLE, MA. 02143

Text font is Vera Sans
Title font is Lydian BT

Acknowledgments:

The author greatly acknowledges the editors of the following publications where these poems first appeared, some in slightly different form:

Apt Magazine: "Sick America"
Down in the Dirt: "An Abstract"
Wilderness House Literary Review:
"*Sparrow*" and ". . .The First Emanation is Light . . ."
Juice Press: "A Walk and Time"
© Mike Amado

Thanks:
With thanks to Harris Gardner for his abundant editing skills.
Sheila M. Twyman for a final proof-read.
My fellow poets, Doug Holder, Gloria Mindock, Ann Carhart, Irene Koronas, Carolyn Gregory, Dorothy Derifield, Marc Widershien, Sandee Storey, Steve Glines, Lo Galluccio, Debbie Priestly, Jack Scully and Walter Howard for showing up at my features.
Thanks to: Afaa Michael Weaver, Dzvinia Orlowsky and Joanna Nealon. Also Barbara Barker of Heartlight Therapies and Teresa Lally of Healing Matters whose treatment and counsel has allowed me to see this book before I wrote it.
And I must not forget to thank my extended poetic family, the BagelBards . . . You guys kick butt!

PREFACE:

This is not a memoir, not meant to diagnose or treat. This is a
path to wellness. I was diagnosed at thirteen with what the med-
ical profession calls, "End Stage Kidney Disease." Eleven years
after which, I've started on dialysis and have been for seven
tough years and counting. In 2002, I received a transplant that
didn't take. This collection maps my journey of taking control
of my health, seeking other, more effective forms of treatment
- and letting healing happen.

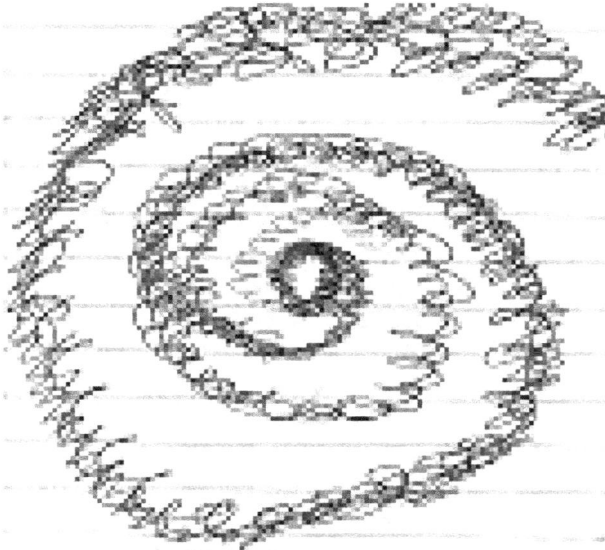

Contents

DIS-EASE

FISTULA SCARS

Cannibal caterpillars crawl
into my arm's flesh
they signal harm below
where the vein was gashed
and given to the artery.
A river bed where dust sleeps,
no blood can thrill -
at one with the streets of Pompeii
my arm is dead.
Vitrified scars that play against the light
adhere to tendons of an arm
taken from a corpse, sewn to a monster
yes this is what I become!
A sum of incisions and death patch-work,
surgeon pelting good will (insult to injury).
The fistula failed while on the table
betadine and cut-marks creep
up my arm again
the second fistula failed
ninety percent mobility replaced
by flood of coagulation.
Incisions sewn with sutures like
lips shut tight on a mouth
that never speaks, sleepy eye sockets
that waken to the blindness of scar tissue

"WELCOME, PATIENT"

a skulking scavenger   so we become

athirst for vicarious *life*   tempting *failure*

it all begins with   a YES   to fear

then   we make eyes   blind to function

only knowing   the machine's hum

and   darkness

when cognition is consigned   cognition gets sliced

patient   screwed   up

impatient   patients   give up

to waiting   and   the duel of inevitable deaths

(*treatment*   or   rejection)

brochures   interpret only   the genuine unreal

where the chronic water-ski

and it's always sunny

TALES FROM THE CHAIR, I
(Ultra Filtration)

Many
times I'd rise
from the chair
to have my sight
swallowed by haze.

Many smiles
in scrubs would say:
You look good   as
self esteem drains
three times a week.

Catheters draw Chi
from body tissues.
Technicians say:
*We're removing excess
fluid, it can kill you.*

Rapidly my will to live
vacuumed away,
my skin an abrasive dust.
I stare down ghosts in
the face of the clock.

My thin bones walk
and end their vigil,
where life dialyses
into the ground.

The world is burned fields,
heavens evaporate,
angels, hit with layoffs,
leap from skyscrapers,
their bodies never found.

TALES FROM THE CHAIR, 2
(The Vibrant and the Dis-eased)

I jerk from the chair after treatment,
then pass out. Come to, gasping:
> *"I'm late for the bus."*
> Five minute walk to the stop,
if bone can melt, my pace is
cold new wax.
> High school tourists with chaperons
> scuff by like toddlers on harnesses.
The gaze of one spears me,
eyebrows lower, grin forms, then he snickers.
> He's seeing the sights.
> Death is not on their itinerary.
Pale skin anxiously hanging in drops as
my slow breath caresses my waning flame.
My hand takes his . . .
> *"Beware, my friend as you pass by . . ."*
> *"In the thick of dying,*
> *you'll fight to live. At least something's*
> *Happening,   how about you?"*
His grip went loose, the skin of
his hand was like a ripe peach.
(I recall that resistant texture).
> If he had seen the day I had . . .
> the hard air opened before me, a bleak
> whirling hollow nailed me to the floor,
> they said I only fainted;
> gave me a cup of water.
> *"How are you doing?"*
> I heard the nurse's wooly shout.
> I thought I saw a warrior brave,
> he had on mourning paint;
> moving slow with a horse
> that had a gouged flank,
> they ghosted into the dark.

13

"JUST WAITING"

Waiting for the Doctor

Waiting for the pills

Waiting for the scalpel

Waiting to heal

Waiting for treatment to begin

Waiting for treatment to end

Waiting to feel better

Waiting to feel worse

Waiting for an organ

Waiting for the worst

Waiting for the ambulance

Waiting for the hearse

GIFT

Leaves splash the hermetic window,
just ancient hands letting go.

My room on the sixth floor,
high enough to see Boston's South-End
and spy on Doctor's private offices.

Days after surgery I'm different.
My johnny with diamond patterns
holds me like smoke.

I want to take-in the warmth
from the window -
the sun doesn't struggle.
An engine baking, a continual
lightning flash, the oven that never cools
during the holidays.

I could've been transplanted
with this star
but . . .

I owe it to the spirit of
the person who
gave this life-article
to me,
to write this down.

KIDNEY TRANSPLANT

This organ, (called cadaveric),
is intention (theirs, more than mine),
am I ready?

Prepped with betadine and warnings,
the release form raises risks,
(Internal bleeding, complications and/or death).

Skin trimmed in the form of archer's bow,
body opened to let in life.
(Immune system crushed by suppressants).

The operation, *a success*
what is four hours, twelve days
to the "rest of my life"?

Warm silence conjures my living fiber.
A stranger's gift sustains me while days grow
malnourished in the fleshed out autumn.

Post-op leaflet discharges euphemisms:
Congratulations on your new life,
New and improved, you're free to go.
"Take at least four to six months, let it heal."

The morning of discharge, Doctor slumps
to the door of my room. He hammers out:
"You never caught Cytomegalovirus, have you?
Well don't. You would die."

Have I fixed my life in hands that shadow
wombs over graves ?

DYING ROAD

I am dreaming of taking myself apart.
It shocks me like shower water
first thing in the morning.
And if I don't write this when I wake
this dream will out-live me . . .

I'm back in high school.
Stuck in a school bus. I sit,
lungs fixed,   no breath.
Mouth shut,   just hardened clay.
Time is a stopwatch kissing a hammer
that pounds back sympathetically.
The autumn gloaming weighs heavy
as the bottom of the sea.
I start to cough, as if air turned to water.
Blood splashes into my hand,
sweatshirt sleeve draws in the red.
It's solid, rounded and furious.
I know what it is -   my own death
for not wanting   my own life.
I ride the dying road with a
blood-pooled hand.

Then I wake up. Skin like a glacier
as I lift out of bed . . .
to the window that held the stars,
frozen as dead wishes.

I start to write:
The Soul . . . the force that can do all but
be put in a bottle is more important than fate.
Let me leave the dying road to recover my Soul.

COMPLICATIONS

My lungs crackle
like infirm lumber.
I don't think this is Bronchitis.
I tell the secretary on the phone.
        I walk to my Doctor's office,
in my ears, winter wind caterwauls
I imagine I'm now immortal.
The waiting room clock asphyxiates
        like a beached whale.
I get to watch a heart patient fighting
in his seat,   reading the same Newsweek.
He glares at his Rolex   every 10.2 seconds.
(I know he was a heart patient from
        his crimson face).
Four hours go,
then I say to the Doctor . . .
        If this is harmony in my body,
        who is the conductor? I drown in discord;
        and my own blood.   Is this a virus marauding?
        Doctor, was I transplanted with a kidney
                or a grenade?
He scribbles on his prescription pad.
His office is on the waterfront
with a full view of
the seafood joints
that close in winter,
and of the steady sea -
ripe with clouds of seaweed.
The Japanese know seaweed
to be a healing algae
that thrives on light.
Doctor hands the prescription
and orders: *You need*
more antibiotics.
    Give me back to the sea.

TO THE WOMB

Anesthesia, Morphine, Demerol chokes
the electricity from my body.   Most counterfeit
of journeys, brought within inches of Acheron
where consciousness dissolves.

Physician smiles back, the light turns black.
Frozen, unconscious, at rest -
I have no coins to place on my lids
to fund final passage.

There runs a river I call sky,
horizon names me. My mind disembarks,
I enter the Earth that I call Mother.
Dry shore soaked by waves.

Mother, my body is scars over scars.
I lay in a medical grave of cold,
white sheets, silent call buttons.
Your song disappears.

Mother, meet me in the water
with my cast-off flesh,
see if we choose to let go

or wake up. Mother,
open me to let in more light.
Your womb shapes snowflake-stars.

Heart wisdom swells in a sliver of a breath,
I now know my name:
I rise on Serpent's head to bring to the sky
the orange crescent amid the webbed stars!

COPING

DOCTOR, DOCTOR -

Assist me in making up my mind.
Go for the jugular?
Or go for Doctor assisted
suicide?
   The bullet and the pill can both
   come to nothing if utilized improperly.
   What are you implying, patient?
    I'm saying: I knew a guy
given six months to live (fifteen years ago)
who had a brain stormed by tumors.
He was given a syringe then told,
"If it comes to this, you know what to do" . . .
   silver pin sends murder bubble
   to pop the balloon of life.
   Patient, are you sure you heard it right?
I did.   But, I need   advice.
No , not on which slow death to commit.
Doctor, assist me
in choosing a full color brochure.
   The one made of photo stock? With high-hair
   centerfolds fully clothed playing
   nurses, with men too late for beer ads,
   too "unathletic" for sneaker selling
   playing patients.

Maybe I'll choose the leaflet carved out of ether,
bathed in rainbow-spheres and moon drops;
breathing silences -
heavy voice commanding
Do not go without wisdom within!
Age-old hands in mudra, a sea mist figure,
seated in lotus, morphs into spider,
into serpent, butterfly then eagle.
May I choose the road that ascends,
self assertive,
but not "sterile" ?
No, you may not.
Like landscaping and plumbing,
medical science is here to provide a service!
All we give is all we have.
    . . . And not all I need.
   My life in medical hands does not demand
   I dream your reality.
   Patient, stop your dreaming,
   fill out this annual smiley-faced survey.
        And on the survey, I wrote
        I have filled up many suggestion boxes
        with dead forests. My T-shirt reads :
        I survived a "failed" transplant
        and all I got was this brochure.

SYSTEMATIC DISPOSAL

Conveyer belt blood smeared
from emergency to back dumpster
Find my racked kidneys there

A maimed arm, black-swollen eyes
gray skin clippings, burned-out heart

took apart
piece by piece

Garbage men turned philanthropic
scavenge my kidneys from the dumpster
a million on the black market

The business grows, thinning the herd
flesh-piles inflamed, bound with dis-ease

they have us
piece by piece

Join what's left with epoxy -
"patient" equals suicide zombie

MYTH

I refuse to believe in feline nature
throwing lives to the wires
like beat-up sneakers.

Bad blood results shovel dirt
on my health, then
I can be resurrected with pills.

I don't believe we can be opened
and closed like empty refrigerators.
And when the priceless fruit perishes,
we can come back for more.

I've heard all the stories:
the grandfather who got a kidney
from his grandson-in-law
and lived,
the husband who gives a kidney
to his wife, or vice-versa,
they both live.
Then there are the ones
who don't make the cut.

But we're all immortal . . .
stories,
            still here.
We are the cats that always come back.

"AN ABSTRACT"

The functional units of the renal organ
exploded in a death-like rot.   I lit the wick.
I held my breath, unraveling afghans in honor
of the new life promised by Doctor Death . . .
Doctor,   blow it out.
Is dis-ease that important
that I should auger bit my brain with fear
and "live" scarred to prove your point?

Too many wrecking balls clog the world
with bombardment. Business as usual
tearing down.
Never loyal to the macro,
disobeying the micro -
tangled flies amid death-web.
Holding back is auto-attack.

Gun goes off . . .
                  off come the gloves,
I found my inner carpenter
and commissioned restoration -
making the solution
out of breaking the problem.
Vicious vistas of human viscousness
are not what I see in wall-cracks . . .
      green valley floor expanding
      extemporaneous flowering
      of yellow-like poppies,
      orange-like yellows,
      watered by pipes piping blood,
      pumping rain and White Light
      that foil the abnormal into fertile soil.
Serving the macro, obeying the micro -
an instrument trained like peripheral eye
    I
      Stain,
           Engage,
                Release.

I'm here for my work.
My life's music -   it's no Opera.
Does it matter not a Sonata ?
Not an opus, but adhesions of a moment?
In three chords,   the rebels' trinity,
a momentary collapse of reason.

(Is one dis-ease more important
than another if both
deliver poems in death-throes ?)
No reason
            exists   to say
               that symptoms exist
                        more than I.

THE FIGURE

A wasted figure ambles the streets,
          scares lost dogs, takes change from the homeless.
He checks his reflection in fast food windows
          and nouveau-riche bistros.
In the bar,
he tells the hip to   *drink up*   and the frat boys to binge.
I see his figure featured in glossy billboards
          constellated with lip glossed girls and hard liquor.
Art imitating life,
                    life imitating
                                        death.
Who is this figure ? ask the masochistic ignorant.
          In every coffee cup-top reeling down the sidewalk
You know he's there,   smiling,   pretty,   pretty pathetic.
Blame away this figure with heredity
                    and getting on in years,
          alleging that the cells commencing rebellion
in the temporal lobe are from mobile phone
radiation and not listening to the Doctor.
                    FEAR is a comfort zone.
And this world stalks   *that*   stalker, too.
                              Not   my   world.
That figure breaks the glass of the car he knows he can steal.
                              Not   my   car.
My headlights on high soak the street,
          alive like an April breeze,
a scent-studded morning.   Life is a shatter of pollen.
Vitality is tailing this Fear Figure,   Declaring:
It's time
          death's shoulder,
                    life's   hand.

A WALK AND TIME

I know I walk with death
three blocks away or three steps behind.
Shadow on my shoulder,   breath on my neck,
he sneaks around in my notebook.

I blow a stalk of air
three life times ahead,
soft down returns to dance
on death's murky sod and burned soil,
blackened out like all my life-lessons that lapsed, unlearned,
distorted into fairytale faster than the shaman shape-shifting
into psychic hotline operator and back again.
Yeah, I invented this legend; and still burning.

From ashes bring ascendancy.

Death, I ask to walk side by side.
I'm purged of playing victim.
MAYBE IT'S YOUR TIME . . .
to admit your rusting scythe
and remit your reign to medicine,
the scalpel and the final rites . . .

(White coats do your job
better with a smile).

Only human death I mean.
No big deal.
Your shoulder   now -
my hand.

MIXED MESSAGES I

A picture in the waiting room:
children feeding woodlarks
by a bird bath.
    Next to it, a memo reads:
    "Patients with coughs
    must wear masks."
The room is full of silent screams.
I think about my native ancestors.
Corn, bean and squash
were their main reserves in summer.
The dietitian chides
    *"These are **the** biggest*
    killers of the End-stage".
Nurses' assistant reads my records. She's baffled
as to why they're thick as a Russian novel -
(for insurance purposes).
Nurses' assistant later blurts out,
"I'm going scuba diving in Aruba this weekend."
    While she inserts a catheter into a man
    numbed by Benadryl.
His voice rests in his pillow.
I stay quiet, hearing everything.
I feel that if they ask me questions
I'll be buried in a paper-blizzard.

MIXED MESSAGES 2

Dying is a masking
more than a wipe-out.
The transplant coordinator says
"A kidney is your best
chance at life,"
Then edits herself . . .
"Everything we'll do for
the kidney is eventually toxic."
What *I* tell my kidneys,
"You are loved, you are needed,
you are welcome".
I harbor darting details of immortality -
pixels concealed by ultrasound.
Like the bottle of iced tea tucked
In my back pack,
(My Doctor demands
that I don't drink fluids),
along with a banana.
The sticker reads
Nourish your body.
Dietitian says:
"Don't eat bananas"

SICK AMERICA:
(A rotting corpse with a fresh dab of lipstick in a
new Lincoln with a handicap plate)

As if car shows in Wally World parking lots aren't bad enough.
My chain-pharmacy now has
ONE THOUSAND NEW BEAUTY PRODUCTS !
Little, furry bunnies and lab rats picket.
And the high glucose walker-brigade already have to sell
their livers for heart pills.
(Maybe sell the Lincoln to purchase new lipstick.)

A big commercial actor says . . .
"I'd tackle the *tough* diseases," but not of course the not-so-tough,
break-your-leg, catch-a-cold dis-eases. They have been conquered
(dust under the rug),   but   not   healed.
Go for the *big ones* first and aim your high-tech guns,
earphones dampen the blast with la-la-la's.
Miss the target, a.k.a **prevention**. No one's listening until too late.
I've seen modern medicine fall on its face
like an asthmatic sales rep receiving CPR
                from a CPR dummy.

Doctor says, *"That's all that can be done now . . .*
take your pills, come back next month."
I aim my big guns: *Doctor, what about AIDS affecting everyone?*
Tumors growing faster than jobs ? Renal patients waiting to fail?
But there are ONE THOUSAND NEW BEAUTY PRODUCTS
                to the band-aid rescue.

My disability check is direct deposited to my pharmacy.
If I can fill up a paper cup with coins I can buy
some new beauty cream to cover up the scars,
the sick eyelids and medical beatings a.k.a, "treatment".
I'm thinking, *"Why do I think this is all my fault?"*
(I expected the "M" word and got the reverse.)
                Get over it !   All of it...
                there is no cure for being human.

"SURVIVAL OF THE FITTEST?"

An autumn weekend with my Native drum group.
Elk skin talks with thunder's cadence.
We sing and pray until the dying sun
lights the leaves shades of citrus and root.
One month after airplanes punctured
the steady morning, buildings buckled.
Still gagging, nation spins in particle clouds.
A phantom fear sprouts from a group member,
pantomime headlines from the Cold War days:
> *"You know, World Trade isn't the last.*
> *We need to save plastic bottles so we can*
> *store water in our basement shelters.*
> *I have a first-aid kit in the car. Sense it in the air?*
> *There are blacker days ahead."*
(Then he puts on a filter mask).

I stay far away
from his new millennium air-raid exercise.
Aside, another member asks me:

> *"If our infrastructure,*
> *with all its goods and services,*
> *were to be wiped out . . .*
> *what are you gonna do?*
> *Build a Dialysis machine*
> *out of reeds and sticks?*
> *Lay in a tub of warm water*
> *with baking soda?*
> *. . . Unlikely."*

Survival,   the understructure of the soul,
shakes and wakes the sleeping colossus
that can save.

My answer:
"Isn't that how we survive?"

HEALING

MY MANTRA

What sustains me?
      It can't be seen.
A temple under water,
a heart that hides hunger.
      A God with a small "g"
that stands as a sculpture
slowly buried by desert
      or volcanic dust.

What sustains me trembles
      with curiosity.
The whistle of a humming bird
and the tongue of a Spider Flower
      in perfect pitch.

What sustains me
      could be a mantra:
"Remember, Transcend, Reclaim, Ascend"
Remember: who you are,
          where you come from.
Transcend: your limitations.
Reclaim: your inner wisdom.
and . . . *Ascend*!

What sustains me
      won't show on the screen
      of a high-tech test.
What sustains me
is my electric body
      blowing whistles.

What is   "to survive" ?
To open both fists, let life fill.
         Cupped hands . . .
the arena of life.

A THREAD OF LIGHT

Up into the star-filled field,
my eyesight unfolds.
I trace the lattice of blue-black night.

High within the vault,   turning -
on the far side the Zenith,   seeking,

between Vega and the pole star is found,
the still-point, the center of eternity

where no light clamors from constellations.

The circle-citadels in ancient lodges
keep watch,   going around
eternity's pillars.

It is here, the Four Guardians
cast not their stare,   the void
opens up and   THE ALL   rains down.

Time runs over the edge of its chalice,
folds under itself in a torus as my heart
ratchets around the Earth's power grid.

Eyes up in gratitude,
eyes cast down in adoration.

Raised by a thread of light,
a black hole in reverse.

"SPARROW"

Nestling child   -
a breeze across the pond,
the life-span of a sparrow,

not a sign of death.

Older now -
lamenting his lost slough,
cry heard by oblivion,

fleeting mark of life.

All things subsist

in the sparrow's dart -

birds dive,   fish leap.

Sparrow's feather falls

onto the pond . . .

a   ripple,

sparrow's   gone.

Child's bones house a heart
that grieves absence.

" . . .THE FIRST EMANATION IS LIGHT . . ."*
*Paraphrase of Paul Foster Case

Dialysis machine
pulses soft light
on walls of my bedroom,
drives fluid into my abdomen.
Pain grips my body python-like.
I wonder :
are deities in the machine?
If so, when the day comes
we all need   pacemakers
will heart then be
divine?   Maybe
people are machines who
need machines. But cells
are micro-Gods.
They thwart the darkness,
this harvest season
that promises burial.
Cells secretly reinvent light.

HEALING TOOLS

Acupuncture,

I.E.T.,

Reiki

echo within me.

Breath work,

Chakras,

Yoga . . .

Prana / Chi
flow within in me.

See me as proof
through healing tools,
not in the mainstream alone
do human beings swim.
This body has rejected
the anchor of disease.

In my body,
Healing
and **balance**
in my body.

Living balance is what I'm
working for.
Resilient far beyond illness,
I endure.

THE 'H' WORD (Healing)

It has been cut, severed, messed up
worse than a plastic surgery accident . . .
erased from our vocabulary, we speak
dead air of sterile hospital rooms.
The "H" word, never sounded,
was written out of its own big budget flick
about a regular man shot down by bad luck
who runs a bike marathon and wins.
He teams up with a young maverick
Doctor with an office full of free samples . . .
which is a front because the doctor's really a spy
with a high-tech gun the size of a blue tooth.
They proceed to save the world from terrorism,
then cure cancer.
The real story is bleak . . .
the sound of rubber wheels
chafe linoleum;
the mop hushes the O.R. floor.
A remorseful dreamer pursues the "H" word
like she's a jaded leading lady. High heels click
through slow-undulating lines in an airport,
dreamer calls leading lady's name.
Leading lady tumbles farther away.
Either dreamer corners her, and they screen-kiss,
or the credits roll.

MANTRA FOR THE BODY OF EARTH

Humans,
           walled cities
on steep mountains
            expecting attack.
The world reflected in my mind,
              I refuse to grow.
A wall tires my heart,
           clotted words brick the light.
Nerves on the defensive,
        defending what?
With each breath,
          light arrives -
with each breath,
          sounds arise -
the
    antonym of Joy
              ceases.
I take my struggle and drop it,
        I hear my mantra and live it.
Deliver the light and be it,
     cleanse the Earth as myself.
        Padlocks mesh my kidneys.
Their keys
        are words:
Allow,   Grace,   Grow,   Peace.

CANCEL CLEAR

Cancel Clear, Cancel Clear.
All negative feelings
and fear . . .   Cancel Clear.
All the thoughts of
"This dis-ease will overtake me"
and "I will die alone."
These thoughts are not my own.
Cancel Clear, Cancel Clear.
All the screams of pain
my body shrills,
only I can hear . . .   Cancel Clear.
All the shades of drowsiness
shrinkwrap my consciousness,
these specters pierce narrow
cracks in idle fences -
these visions are not my own.
I am where expansion grows.
Cancel Clear, Cancel Clear
so that I may get there . . .
to the mirror in the abyss,
rise beyond the fence,
that barrier of despair
between here and there,
the shore and the sea,
spirit and body,
hand and wand,
mind and heart -
so I may shout back at the
world of sick-vulgar-blindness:
Cancel Clear! Cancel Clear!

CALLING BACK

Calling back my spirit,
calling back my soul,
calling back the pieces
that I let go
to the world, to people
that I know and don't know,
I rive myself open then
split my self to slivers
as a fractured mannequin China doll.
Left wide open to the world and
illusions, commanding:
"Come forward, Take your fill!"
and infiltrate my soul.
NO - a thousand mantras NO,
higher self can't be overthrown.
Unknotted pieces discarded
that I lent on lease
are returning to me times three.
Blessed Be!
Acceptance of Process,
a vibe of Ease
and Personal Power
continually flows.
My entity vibrates
in tune with the euphony of
healing energy.
Blessed Be!
Calling back my spirit,
calling back my soul,
reconnecting the pieces,
connecting the WHOLE.

SUMMONED GEOMETRY

Within the body   I am the bones,
Without the body   I am the soul.
Inside the torso,
I am the spine,
Inside the circle,
I am the line.
Inside the cup   I am the swirling,
Outside the flower   I am the petal.
Outside the circle,
I am the square,
Outside the circle,
The triangle . . .
The ellipse of mother keeping child,
Angle of the lotus pose,
The infinity-eight of moving lovers,
The coil of clasping hands . . .
The unbent column of
Rushing warriors with
Gust of lions roaring
From their throats,
The rise of the lungs as
They gather the air,
Cathedral's vault and
The muscle of hymns.
So creation sings
Woven with strings,
Energy woven tight unravels
On healing wings.
Inside, let BALANCE begin,
Inside, let BALANCE sustain;
In every system and cell
All WILL be well.
Be still . . .
Be still . . .
And know.

BODY TO PERSONAL POWER

The brain,
        the heart
                ventricles
are the spiral of a shell -
sanctuary,   unity,
fused in strength.

I'm being a spiral being,
revolving,   evolving
without fear,   moving.
Centered . . .
Not a clone of symptoms proliferating palsy,
ignoring the flow of the Kundalini
which twists in Fierce Joy, a taper writhing
in the tight-rope winds. Every time we sneeze
we break another link in the chain of dead beliefs.
I don't believe I'm only my body
but in a body that dies
we wait   and want   to stagnate.
Time to heal disconnect.

My walled city melts
with the impact of gentle down,
Gratitude
                spirals
                        outward.

Sea shells whirl with   Gratitude,
galaxies turn with   Gratitude
scattering Sacred Geometries.

"CONTEMPLATION"

I contemplate my situation
by studying the refrigerator
light: when opened, it's on
            when closed, it's off
just like my mind. I choose
this instant, this moment to be
utterly overt.
I contemplate
until my skin casts back a thousand
reflections: which one is me?
                    which one is you?
Everyone who sees
themself in you
are overcoats of chrome
polished by others envy.
A clouded mind is a soiled sky,
clouds make slivers of stars and
stagnant energy slows down the body
until all that's left is malady. . .
and death.
One body   contains my one brain
            that isn't one at all.
            Layers overlap on layers,
            various facets flow like
color from a faucet, a liquid Rubik's Cube.
Many sides to one personality,
no need to match the colored squares.
(And no, right now I am not on acid).
    Consciousness provides
    an escape-hatch
a latent capacity to walk out of this brain
like quitting a job.

So I shake up my head,   pop the cork,
let my Higher Self mingle
with the Divine Everywhere
in a transcendental water tornado.
My psyche slips like a bendy straw
into that bottle that's more
            full than I am.
    There is a part of the human vehicle
    that Dr. Mechanics can't remove,
THAT'S THE PART I LIVE FROM.
The Creator doesn't create imperfection,
perfection lives in acceptance.
We live in an altruistic universe -
THAT'S MY ALTERNATE REALITY.
No galaxy is malformed;
even trampled flowers pose with dignity.
    I have shed all hostility
    to fire, cut by the blade of life,
yet that umbilical cord is unbroken
climbing sky-bound like ignited fireworks
touching the beat of the arterial sky
giving birth to flame and flower burst.
"I Have Seen the Light and it is My Mind"
it shines: tones of subtlety,
                tiffany lotus petals,
unfold circular haloes like
hooded cobras,   up through
the stratosphere
        WITH NOTHING TO FEAR.
    I jump out of myself,
fill the Grand Canyon,
feel the vastness envelope me
until "me" is greater than myself.
I'm not as big as I thought.
        I persist in human form,
        an   arrow   of   light.

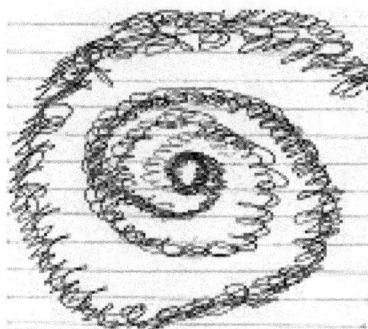

Glossary

"'DIS-EASE' : The body's natural state is to be at ease.
Illness occurs when total being moves away from persona,
becomes the symptoms of illness it is experiencing,
and lives the 'disease' that has manifested.
Dis-ease is the body simply out of sync with self."   - B. G. B.

Fistula: Also known as an arteriovenous fistula or "Hemo dialy-
sis access". A vein attached to the artery, usually in the arm as
an entrance into the bloodstream. This access is used cnly for
hemo dialysis.

Ultra Filtration: A term used for the process of remov ng
excess fluid from the body during dialysis treatment.

Reiki: Generally a hand's on method of energy work.
Bringing in Universal Energy to assist in the healing process.
This energy "goes where it is needed" in the body to correct
many health conditions.

Paul Foster Case: (10/3/1884 - 3/2/1954) A foremost American
occultist and author. His writings on the Tarot ard Kabbala
became the lessons for members of the Builders of the Adytum
(B.O.T.A.).

I.E.T. : Integrated Energy Therapy. Working with the nire angels
in specific areas of the body to release emotional situations that
accumulate in the body.

"Cancel, Clear": computerese. Cancel means to stop
an application, Clear means to clear it away.

MIKE AMADO is a performance poet, a drummer and percussionist born and raised in Plymouth Massachusetts. He published his first volume of verse in 2006. In 2008, "Stunted In-ner-child Shot the TV" (High-risk Spoken Word) was published by Cervena Barva Press. His work has appeared in many magazines and online journals. He is the co-founder of "Poetry: The Art of Words" a monthly poetry reading and open mic in Plymouth, Ma. Amado is a dialysis "patient" and a "failed" transplant recipient. His medical poems weigh the pros and cons of treat-ment while *illustrating the power of the mind and strength of the spirit.*

Photo by Jack Scully